things i'm dying to move on from

Robert Mason

BookLeaf
Publishing

India | USA | UK

Presentation by *BookLeaf Publishing*

Web: www.bookleafpub.com

E-mail: info@bookleafpub.com

ISBN: 9789360941956

First edition 2024

ACKNOWLEDGEMENT

I acknowledge Jesus of Nazareth as the Christ, the Son of the living God

PREFACE

The following is a collection of (mostly) unfinished or abandoned writings transcribed from my journals or wrote down spontaneously, usually during times of extreme stress. They are in no particular order, and presented without context.

Swept away by your waves
You pull me further from your shores
Begging me to explore your depths
As water fills my lungs

Endless chatter about nothing
Broken by the futility of my pleas
I'm drowning in you
But I still haven't gotten your attention yet

The weight of your world crashes down
And squeezes the last bit of magic from my
chest
It's time to dive down and embrace monotony
I'm surrounded by you but I still feel nothing

And now the storm has passed
All the birds have fallen from the sky and
drowned
Behind me I take another look and see you,
The shore I used to call home

2

You taste like tangerines
Your skin is so hard to penetrate
But to taste your flesh is worth the pain
I want to feel your acid on my lips
I want to feel your burn
I wouldn't even mind if you cut me on the way
down
As long as you promise to enter my veins softly
I hope the taste lingers for eternity
Existing
Dissipating slowly
Becoming one with me
Because once your sweetness is gone
All I'm left with is
Your ugly
Bitter
Skin

3

She was always so human. So real. So close, yet she paid little attention to anything going on around her. She was so far away, her eyes locked onto her empty notebook. She held an entire universe within her eyes, but I couldn't access it. I wasn't the object of her gaze, or her desire.

Every now and then her face would light up with excitement, and she seemed as though she was about to speak something profound. But instead of using words, she only spoke with her pen on the page of that old and purple notebook.

What did she have to say? If it was for me to know, she would have told me. Instead she wrote, presumably to herself only and for herself only. It was evidently what brought her the most joy in life, as I never had felt such peace radiate from her as when he became lost in that secret universe again and spoke into the pages with her pen.

And yet, I've come to regard those moments as not happy after all. Because the next time I would see her she was back to her old ways.

Quiet. Not just to this world but her's as well. A blank expression on her face that matched the blank pages of her book. Whatever was written there the previous day had been torn out and presumably discarded. Whatever she had spoke on to those pages had become lost, like spoken words disappearing into the air.

I wonder what the point of all this was. If you didn't care for permanence, why use a pen? If you didn't want this world to remember what you spoke, why not use your voice to write instead? Let my ears be the paper you used to write your story. These words you say, they too will become lost memories, with no tearing of pages required. Everything becomes a lost memory eventually, with no intervention needed.

5

I was your rock, but I told you not to trust me

I crumbled so easily under the pressure of you asking for the bare minimum

And now we're both stuck here, alone and still together

I'm crushing you underneath the weight of this disappointment, but I'm the one who can't breathe

You look so pretty when we're both choked up

I love your many faces. As long as we never meet I don't have to pick just one. You'll never have to know that I'm barely even human these days. I'll never have to explain away my past or make excuses. I will never get the chance to break your heart or hear what your voice sounds like when it breaks. You will never know the disaster that I am. Oh love, what a beautiful disaster we could have been together. If only I hated you enough to ask for your name

6

I paint your picture
On my wall
I hear you scream
My name for all

I close my eyes
It never stops
I feel you as
Your bottle drops

And empty on
The windowsill
Another bottle
Of someone's pills

I stretch my voice
Across the room
From the corner I see
Your flower bloom

Without me you're
Devoid of shame
Devoid of comfort
Devoid of pain

Who is it that answers when you call out to a
false god?
I made my own decisions but I always picked
the wrong one

And who is it that calls out when your inner
voice becomes lost?
I hear a hundred souls but I don't recognize a
single one

Every single second is another minute wasted
I reach my hands for love but pain was only
what I tasted

I'm still making my decisions and I don't think
that I'll make it
I'll never know the answers but dear God, I'm
gonna face it

8

Inside my head lives memories
The way things were and how they'll be
Saviors come and saviors flee
You love them all but never me
Surround yourself with this new scene
The people that I'll never be
The feelings I will never be
The sights that I will never see
The sights that you will always see
I'm not the one you wanna see
Just cast me out and you'll be free
And in the end what will I be?
A haunted house for you and me

I don't remember which promises I never meant
to keep
And which ones I gave up on keeping along the
way
I am a cry for help,
Waiting to shut my mouth at any response
I don't know what I'm begging you for anymore
If I feel like starving myself,
It's because I'm hungry

10

You keep your medicine
In your arm
And on your tongue
Your magic charms
You lost your wristwatch
There's no alarm
The sky turns pink
There's no alarm

11

Defuse me

If you don't want to know

If you can learn to live without me

Defuse me

I don't care

If you have to quench this flame in your blood

Defuse me

Taking you down with me

Was never my idea of together forever

Defuse me

Please

I don't want to leave you in this world alone

12

Do you remember when

We ate that box of lemon cookies on your
boyfriend's bed

You told him we were just friends

I didn't know how to pretend

We both knew how we wanted that night to end

But now I'll never eat lemon cookies with you
again

13

A man walks into his kitchen to grab a beer

He sits on the couch with the TV on

He looks at his dog and asks

"So, this is it?"

The dog doesn't reply

The man smiles at the ceiling, closes his eyes
and says

"So this is it"

15

This is not a poem

Nor a cry for help

I hate writing poetry

And I hate crying

But I'll do whatever it takes

To make you finally listen to me

15

I climbed over you while you slept

And let out my blood as I wept

Letting go of the youth that I kept

I'm asking the mirror what's next

16

The only glimpse I get of you is from my
dreams

Your skin feels so cold

And your voice so quiet

Maybe it's because dead women don't talk

Suddenly I remember

Nightmares are dreams too

17

Do you think you're pretty in blue

Because you're the only one with new flesh

Well honey, I have just as many skeletons as you

And if you ask me, I swear you'll never get rest

18

How does it feel
To build somebody up with sand
Instead of teaching them to build with stone?

To build me up with borrowed time
With futile dreams on empty beaches
And lies of memories you knew we'd never
make

Does it make you happy
To tell me to walk on water
Even though you're the one pulling me under?

At the bottom of this sea
When I've been dissected by all my fears
Maybe I'll be light enough to fly again

But for now I fall
And I love the sounds the waves make
And I love the feeling of falling

I love the feeling of falling in love
With falling out of love with you

Appendix I: Opus of Infamy

I've suffered through seven summers

Becoming frostbitten from the motionless snow
the false sun refused to melt, I realized my lungs
were for water and not air

Four angels approached me as I stood alone and
frozen in time for fourteen years

They had mirrors for faces and each reflected a
different horror. I responded to their gaze by
tossing stones until they shattered and pierced
my chest

I expelled the contents of my heart and stomach
onto countless pages and phone screens until I
was the only one who could read the message

I've survived through seven summers

Appendix II: The Bluejay

21

I'm finally alive
I hear the world come awake outside
And birds are coming in through the open
window
They're singing songs for only me

I'm older now
I know birds sing for all of us
Except for bluejays
Bluejays sing songs for only me

Appendix III: The End of Things

It's time

To take advantage of

This newfound weightlessness

I was never strong enough

To carry the world on my shoulders

But that's no excuse

To give up on

Carrying myself

But this time

Instead of

Dragging my cold and lifeless body

Into the ground

I think

I'll carry myself

To church

And to the doctor

And to my grandma's house

And I think I'll like to read again

And I think I'll watch movies again

And I think I'll like to live again

And I think I'll like to love again

And all of that starts now

With loving myself

With a love that is

Sensitive

Active

Genuine

Eternal